American Moments

ABDO
& Daughters

THE BOSTON TEA PARTY

By Cory Gunderson

VISIT US AT
WWW.ABDOPUB.COM

Published by ABDO Publishing Company, 4940 Viking Drive, Suite 622, Edina, Minnesota 55435. Copyright ©2004 by Abdo Consulting Group, Inc. International copyrights reserved in all countries. No part of this book may be reproduced in any form without written permission from the publisher.

Printed in the United States.

Edited by: Sheila Rivera
Contributing Editor: Kate A. Conley
Cover Design: Mighty Media
Interior Design and Production: Terry Dunham Incorporated
Photos: Corbis, Library of Congress

Library of Congress Cataloging-in-Publication Data

Gunderson, Cory Gideon.
    The Boston Tea Party / Cory Gunderson.
       p. cm. -- (American moments)
    Summary: Discusses how and why American colonists protested high taxes from Great Britain by dumping tea in Boston harbor in 1773, as well as the ramifications of their actions. Includes bibliographical references (p.) and index.
    Contents: Setting the stage -- A struggle for power -- Resisting royal control -- The Boston Tea Party--The King responds -- The push for independence.
    ISBN 1-59197-280-9
    1. Boston Tea Party, 1773--Juvenile literature. [1. Boston Tea Party, 1773. 2. United States--History--Revolution, 1775-1783--Causes.] I. Title. II. Series.

E215.7.G86 2004
973.3'115--dc21
                                                                                  2003057816

CONTENTS

SETTING THE STAGE

The night of December 16, 1773, was rainy and cold in Boston Harbor. About 150 boys and men darkened their faces with burnt cork. They wrapped themselves in blankets and stuck feathers in their hair. Disguised as Mohawk Native Americans, they divided into three groups. One by one, the men climbed on board three East India Company ships.

For more than a month, these British-owned ships had sat in the harbor. Each was filled with crates of tea leaves ready to be unloaded. The British government had assumed that the cargo would be delivered to Boston merchants. The colonial merchants were then to pay the British government a tea tax. The colonists resented the tax on the tea leaves. They were boycotting to make their resentment known.

Quickly and quietly, the men on the ships swung their axes to split open the crates. Four hours later, all 23,000 pounds (10,433 kg) of tea were thrown overboard into the water. From shore, members of Britain's Royal Navy and hundreds of Boston colonists watched the protest unfold. The colonists cheered. Members of the navy did not even try to stop the destruction. They feared that bystanders could get hurt if they used their guns to stop the protesters.

The protest became known as the Boston Tea Party. It was the first major protest by the colonists against the British government. This event helped set the stage for the American Revolutionary War.

American colonists cheer as protesters dressed as Mohawk Native Americans throw tea from British East India Company ships.

Boston Harbor had a rich history even before the protests in 1773. Historians estimate that Native-American tribes settled and traded in the area for at least 4,000 years before the Massachusetts Bay Company arrived in the early 1600s. The Native Americans collected clams from the shores of Boston Harbor and caught flounder, cod, and mackerel from the sea.

When Europeans later settled in the area, they took full advantage of the harbor. Boston became the busiest seaport in the colonies. By the 1700s, Boston became a world leader in shipbuilding. It also became the largest and busiest cargo port in America.

ESTABLISHMENT OF THE COLONIES

The British government and the colonists were not always at odds. For more than 100 years, their relationship had been cooperative. The British government had encouraged the establishment of American colonies.

From the sixteenth to the eighteenth centuries, powerful European countries operated under an economic policy called mercantilism. Each country focused on building its wealth. Each country tried to export as many products as it could to earn money. The European empires did not want to import any more products than necessary. Importing cost them money, while exporting made money.

Under mercantilism, empires saw the conquering of other lands as another way to increase their wealth. Colonizing new territories opened up new markets for export goods. The journey to new territories created new trade routes. It was also a way to increase European empires' physical presence and power.

The first permanent British colony was established in Virginia in 1607. Great Britain's King James I granted the Virginia Company the right to establish the colony. The Virginia Company of London was organized and funded by British merchants. The company sold

British merchant ships approach Jamestown, Virginia.

stock, which allowed it to buy the ships and supplies the colonists needed. These merchants hoped the colonists would find precious metals and other raw materials in America, which could be sold in England. These sales would result in profits for the merchants who invested in the company.

Many people who later ventured to America went so they could worship freely. In England, the only religious denomination people were allowed to belong to was the Church of England. In the colonies, they weren't forced to belong to any specific church. By 1732, the British government had established 13 colonies in North America. These colonies stretched along the Atlantic coast from Canada to Florida.

THE THIRTEEN COLONIES

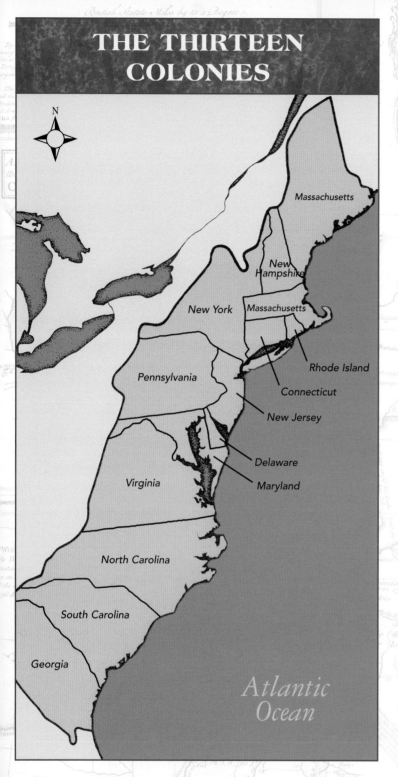

N

Massachusetts

New Hampshire

New York

Massachusetts

Rhode Island

Connecticut

New Jersey

Pennsylvania

Delaware

Maryland

Virginia

North Carolina

South Carolina

Georgia

Atlantic Ocean

The British East India Company handled trade between England and the colonies. It was a joint-stock organization similar to the Virginia Company. These companies, and others like them, were funded by groups of owners who invested money in them. The money earned from these investments was shared among the owners.

The British Empire also made money from the colonies by taxing the colonists. In the seventeenth century, British parliament had passed laws that gave it control over the colonies' international trading. These laws were called the Navigation Acts. They forbade the colonies from selling their products to any country but England. In addition, any foreign products the colonies imported had to first pass through England so Parliament could charge taxes on them.

Parliament established the trade rules to benefit England's economy. For almost 100 years, the colonists did not voice objection to them. They worked around some of the rules by breaking British laws. Smuggling became a common way for the colonists to avoid paying taxes on goods from other countries.

For many years, British kings and queens ignored the illegal trading. While it wasn't written, they had a policy of salutary neglect. This meant that they did not enforce the laws that were created to keep the colonies under England's economic control.

The informal policy of salutary neglect ended during King George III's reign. King George III ruled Great Britain and Ireland from 1760 until 1820. During his reign, the British Empire competed with other empires for world domination.

Unlike the British kings and queens before him, King George III wanted tight control over the colonies. He began to impose strict laws on the colonists. These laws triggered confrontations between the colonists and the British government. The confrontations united the colonists and transformed them into revolutionaries. They ultimately resulted in the colonies' independence from England.

KING GEORGE III

King George III was born in 1738, nearly a decade after the original 13 colonies were established in America. Beginning in 1760, he ruled England for almost 60 years. His reign was the second longest in British history. The king suffered with bouts of madness caused by the disease porphyria. Some of these bouts impacted his ability to rule the British Empire. When King George III died in 1820, he was blind, deaf, and mentally ill.

A STRUGGLE FOR POWER

From 1754 to 1763, Native-American warriors sided with the French military in battling British and colonial forces in the French and Indian War. Both sides fought for control of North American land. The British troops and American colonial militia defeated the French and the Native Americans.

Great Britain's victory meant that it was now the most powerful empire in the world. The British Empire had colonies on almost every continent. It was costly to run the vast empire. In addition, Great Britain had also taken on great debt from its involvement in the war.

The British Empire was in serious economic trouble. To help pay some of these debts, King George III and the British parliament imposed new taxes on the colonists. They felt the colonies should help cover the cost of the war. After all, the British military support during the French and Indian War kept the French from taking over the colonists' land in America.

The 1764 American Revenue Act was the first law passed by Parliament specifically to raise money from the colonies for England. It became known as the Sugar Act. New or higher taxes were placed on sugar, textiles, wine, coffee, and indigo imported from markets

DID YOU KNOW?

Before George Washington became the first president of the United States, he played an important role in the French and Indian War. Washington sided with the British and the colonists against the French and the Indians. The two sides fought for control over trade and settlement rights to the upper Ohio River valley.

On October 31, 1753, the twenty-one-year-old Washington was sent to the Ohio River valley by Governor Dinwiddie with a letter for the French. The letter ordered the French to leave the area. Even though the French refused to leave, the House of Burgesses rewarded Washington for his service to the colony.

Washington was later promoted to lieutenant colonel. He and his troops were forced to surrender to the French after a day-long battle on July 3, 1754. This battle marked the beginning of the French and Indian War.

Washington was released as part of the surrender agreement. Upon his return to the colonies, he wrote a letter to the House of Burgesses. In it, Washington thanked the House of Burgesses for their support of him and his troops. The letter also expressed his hope that his future conduct would be deserving of their appreciation.

Top: *George Washington poses in the White House.*

Right: *A copy of the letter that George Washington wrote to the House of Burgesses on October 23, 1754*

outside of Great Britain. Customs laws were also changed to prevent molasses from being smuggled into the colonies.

When governments put sales tax on goods, they force citizens to pay extra money for the products they buy. The money is typically used to provide services to its citizens. The colonists resented giving up part of their income to Parliament. Parliament included representatives from all of Great Britain's countries. However, the American colonies had no representatives in Parliament.

Colonists did not think it was fair to pay taxes to a government in which they had no input. The taxes created an economic crisis for the colonies. The colonists were angry. They voiced their dissatisfaction as "no taxation without representation."

The colonists began to correspond with one another. A group of men in Boston formed the first Committee of Correspondence in 1764. This committee wrote to the citizens of other colonies. It encouraged the colonists to unite and oppose Parliament's tight control over them.

Colonists in many cities agreed to stop buying British products. Some colonial politicians complained to Parliament. They said that the Sugar Act hurt their businesses. Not only did Parliament ignore the colonists and politicians' complaints, it handed down yet another tax.

In March 1765, Parliament passed the Stamp Act. This act taxed public papers such as newspapers, licenses, playing cards, pamphlets, and legal deeds. Even papers sold within the colonies were taxed. Once the colonists paid the tax on the papers, they were supposed to put a stamp on them. This was proof of payment. The money the government collected from the taxes was used to help maintain British troops in the American colonies. It was also imposed to help reduce England's debt from the French and Indian War.

The colonists were furious. This was the first time the British government taxed goods that were traded within the colonies. Patrick Henry, a colonist from Virginia, led a fight to protest the Stamp Act. Newspapers in the colonies published Henry's call to disobey the British government. Colonists who were loyal to King George III accused Henry of treason.

On June 2, 1765, the British government passed the Quartering Act. This act required the colonists to provide British soldiers with food, transportation, and places to live. The British parliament reasoned that the soldiers were protecting the colonists from the French. Members of Parliament felt that it was reasonable for the colonists to support the soldiers. But the colonists didn't feel threatened by the French, and they resented having to support the British military presence in the colonies.

Patrick Henry urged colonists to challenge the Stamp Act.

Protests against the acts of Parliament united some colonists. Throughout the colonies, many people met in secret. Together, street mobs and city leaders planned ways to oppose the new taxes. These rebel colonists called themselves the Sons of Liberty. In Boston alone, nearly 300 colonists were members of this resistance group. Some were printers, carpenters, and blacksmiths. Others were businessmen and doctors.

Members of the Sons of Liberty belonged to the Whig Party. The Whigs wanted to limit Britain's control of the colonies. They believed that the colonies should be independent of the British government. Meanwhile, members of the Tory Party were loyal to the British government. Tories wanted to help preserve Parliament's control over the colonies.

Boston colonists protest the Stamp Act.

The Sons of Liberty moved the colonists into action. They explained why the taxes were unjust. They united the colonists and encouraged riots of protest.

Many colonists got out of paying the stamp tax by avoiding businesses that required it. The Sons of Liberty put pressure on the stamp agents, the British officials whose jobs were to collect the tax. Sometimes the rebels even used violence against the stamp agents. Across the colonies, most citizens refused to pay the tax. By the fall of 1765, all the agents had quit their jobs.

Another response to the Stamp Act was the formation of the New York Committee of Correspondence. This committee kept all colonies updated on the actions it took to resist the Stamp Act. In October 1765, nine colonies sent delegates to New York. The 27 delegates attended a meeting called the Stamp Act Congress. They met for 18 days to plan their protest of the tax.

The Stamp Act Congress passed the Declaration of Rights and Grievances. The declaration stated that the colonists had the same rights as British citizens. The delegates told the British government that only leaders elected by the colonists could tax the colonists. Many business owners applied more pressure by agreeing not to buy British goods until the Stamp Act was eliminated.

Meanwhile in England, many British business people told Parliament of their lost income. The British government decided that it could not enforce the Stamp Act. By March 1766, the Stamp Act was repealed.

The colonists rejoiced over the repeal of the Stamp Act. The repeal meant that the colonists' protests had paid off. The colonists fired cannons, set off fireworks, rang church bells, and hung lanterns

The Liberty Tree was used as a rebelling point. It was more than 120 years old when British soldiers cut it down in 1775. It yielded 14 cords of firewood. That's almost 1,800 cubic feet (51 cubic meters) of wood!

on the Liberty Tree, an elm tree in Boston where colonists met to stage protests.

With the repeal of the Stamp Act, the Sons of Liberty accomplished its goal. The group stopped meeting. But the seeds of rebellion had been sown.

However, Great Britain's economic problems continued. On the same day that the Stamp Act was repealed, the British government adopted the Declaratory Act. This act stated that the British government had the right to tax and make laws for the American colonies. By passing the Declaratory Act, the British government asserted its control over the colonies.

Charles Townshend was a British official in charge of the empire's treasury. In 1767, he drafted a plan to get more money from the colonies. He introduced a new set of taxes, which were called the Townshend duties. They were a part of the Townshend Acts.

There were several measures under the Townshend Acts. One was the Revenue Act. Under this act, paper, tea, lead, paint, and glass were taxed. Colonists were allowed to import these products only from Great Britain. The Townshend Acts also established customs commissioners in the colonies to ensure that taxes were collected.

In response to imposed taxes, American colonists tar and feather a British tax collector.

These taxes were different than other taxes imposed by Parliament. They didn't just tax American imports from foreign countries, but they taxed imports from Great Britain, too. The taxes were also different because they went toward a specific cause. They were used to pay the salaries of the colonies' royal governors.

Until the Townshend Acts, the colonial governments paid royal governors directly. Now Parliament intended to collect taxes and pay the governors itself. Colonists worried that the governors would then favor Parliament, which paid their salaries. British leaders thought the colonists would accept this indirect tax. They couldn't have been more wrong.

By 1767, colonial leaders Samuel Adams, his cousin John Adams, and Patrick Henry were motivating their fellow colonists. They alerted their countrymen that the colonies' right to self-govern was at stake. Colonial politicians joined the protest. The New York legislature refused to provide housing for British troops. The Massachusetts legislature convinced other colonies to boycott British goods.

Parliament responded by dismissing the Massachusetts and New York legislatures. The dismissals convinced the colonists that they had been right about Parliament's intent to control them.

George Washington was one colonist intent on self-governing. He said, "At a time when our lordly Masters in Great Britain will be satisfied with nothing less that the [loss] of American freedom, it seems highly necessary that something should be done to . . . maintain the liberty which we had derived from our ancestors. . . . Yet arms [declaring war] should be the last resort."

John Adams was born in the Massachusetts Bay Colony. He was a key leader in the rebellion against England. In 1797, he became the second president of the United States.

RESISTING ROYAL CONTROL

By 1768, in response to the Townshend Acts, the Sons of Liberty began to meet again. Members communicated with each other across the colonies. Their goals were to unite and resist British control. In Boston, they hung dummies that looked like the British customs commissioners from the Liberty Tree.

Colonists banded together. They refused to shop in stores that imported British goods. Mobs of colonists bothered shop owners and at times resorted to violence. Colonists threw stones and snowballs at people who sided with Parliament.

Massachusetts's governor grew worried about the violence. He asked Parliament to send troops to the colonies. He hoped the British troops would protect royal officials and control the mobs.

On October 1, 1768, a British warship arrived in Boston Harbor. Soldiers carrying bayonets attached to their guns marched into town. This made the colonists of Boston furious. The colonists despised the soldiers. The soldiers were seen as a constant reminder of Great Britain's desire to control them.

The soldiers patrolled day and night, sometimes taunting the colonists. The colonists called the soldiers "lobster backs" because of the red coats they wore. It was not unusual for fistfights to break out between the soldiers and colonists.

British soldiers arrive in Boston Harbor on naval ships. They came to help maintain order among the angered American colonists.

On March 5, 1770, the violence between the two groups turned deadly. Nearly 12 inches (30 cm) of snow had fallen that day. In the evening, a mob of about 100 men and boys began throwing snowballs at soldiers who were standing near the State House. Insults were thrown back and forth between the two groups.

The soldiers were not allowed to shoot their guns unless their captain gave the order. Even though no order was given, a soldier fired into the mob of civilians. Eight soldiers fired after him. By the time the soldiers' captain was able to stop the shooting, five colonists were killed and others were wounded. This attack on the colonists by British soldiers became known as the Boston Massacre. The tension had neared its boiling point.

British soldiers fire at American colonists during the Boston Massacre.

The British immediately tried to downplay the situation. The colonists were furious. They threatened to retaliate against the British soldiers for the attack. Lieutenant Governor Thomas Hutchinson wanted to bring peace to the situation. He moved the British troops out of Boston. He sent them to stay on an island in the nearby harbor.

British soldiers who took part in the Boston Massacre were eventually brought to trial. Colonists John Adams and Josiah Quincy volunteered to defend the British soldiers. They did this to show the British that their soldiers could receive a fair trial in a colonial court. During the trial, the prosecution had very little evidence to support its case. Seven British soldiers were cleared of any crime. One of these men was Captain Thomas Preston, the man in charge of the British troops at the Boston Massacre.

Two of the other British soldiers were found guilty of manslaughter. This charge was less severe than a murder charge. Many colonists disagreed with the court's decisions. Yet, the trial and the governor's removal of British troops from Boston eased tension between the British and the colonists.

The relationship between the American colonists and the British Empire improved. In April 1770, the British Empire abolished most of the Townshend Acts. By doing away with these acts, the British government removed or lessened many of the sales taxes that the colonists were required to pay.

Only the taxes on tea remained the same. The colonists' anger over the tea tax would lead to conflict and eventually to a revolution.

THE BOSTON TEA PARTY

The East India Company had been chartered by Queen Elizabeth I in 1600. The organization permitted Great Britain to participate in the spice trade. The British parliament controlled the company.

In May 1773, the British parliament passed the Tea Act. The goal of the act was to support the East India Company, which was struggling financially. The company was in debt. It also owned more than 18 million pounds (8,164,656 kg) of unsold tea. The sale of this tea could save the company from financial ruin.

Some members of British parliament had invested in the East India Company. They wanted to make money on their investment by increasing tea sales.

The British government said the East India Company did not have to pay any taxes on the tea it shipped to the American colonies. This enabled the company to sell its tea for less than the colonial merchants could sell it.

Even though the Tea Act would allow the colonists to pay less for their tea, they didn't like this arrangement. The act forbade them buying tea from anyone other than the East India Company. They felt the deal was unfair to the colonial merchants. Colonists worried that these rules might be extended to other products, too. If that happened, merchants could possibly lose their businesses.

The colonists had had enough. They were tired of the taxes and regulations the British government imposed on them. They did not want to receive future shipments from the company ships.

The colonists planned their response to the Tea Act. An angry crowd gathered at the Old South Meetinghouse in Philadelphia. The group passed a resolution condemning the act. Colonists said the act was an attack "upon the liberties of America which every American was in duty bound to oppose."

Three East India Company ships, named *Dartmouth*, *Eleanor*, and *Beaver,* arrived in Boston to unload their tea. Colonists prevented the ships' crews from unloading the tea as planned. The colonists weren't sure what to do about the ships. They knew that the longer they forced the ships to remain in the water, the angrier Parliament would get.

The colonists made their stand on December 16, 1773. The disguised colonists threw 342 cases of tea into the ocean. The Boston Tea Party resulted in the destruction of $16,000 worth of tea leaves.

THE KING RESPONDS

The Boston Committee of Correspondence recorded what happened during the tea party. News of the event spread quickly throughout the colonies. This was due to in large part to Paul Revere. Revere was one of the disguised colonists who took part in the tea rebellion. On December 17, 1773, he rode his horse to New York and Philadelphia. He shared the Committee of Correspondence report with colonists in those cities.

The report said that the tea had not been destroyed solely to avoid the tea tax. Instead, members of the Committee of Correspondence said they destroyed the tea to teach the British a lesson. The British had to learn that the colonists would no longer tolerate any type of taxation without representation.

The success of the Boston Tea Party inspired other colonists to pursue similar actions. A ship named the *London* came to New York on April 22, 1774, with a cargo of tea leaves. A mob of colonists boarded the ship. They destroyed all of the tea leaves on board.

On October 15, 1774, the *Peggy Stewart* sailed into Annapolis Harbor in Maryland. The colonists were angered by the discovery of more than 2,300 pounds (1,043 kg) of tea on board the ship. Captain Anthony Stewart feared what the colonists might do to his family. He apologized, but it did no good. In an attempt to make

Paul Revere was not only a patriot and special messenger between colonies, he was also a silversmith. Revere also designed a Boston Massacre monument and the Massachusetts state seal. The seal is still used by Massachusetts today.

Angry American colonists capture a British tax collector.

peace, Stewart sailed the ship out in front of the town. There he set it on fire. The tea never reached the Maryland shore.

Colonists also boycotted the tea that did make it ashore. The goal behind these boycotts was to harm the British financially. The colonists felt that if they could do this, then perhaps the British would pay attention to the colonists' complaints. The British might even treat the colonists more fairly. Because of the rebellion and the boycotts, many British ships returned home without unloading any of their cargo.

The British didn't like any of the colonists' rebellious actions. In 1774, Parliament implemented a series of acts that were designed to make the colonists obey British laws. The colonists called these the Intolerable Acts because they could not and would not tolerate them.

The first of the Intolerable Acts was the Boston Port Act. Both houses in the British parliament passed the act quickly. It became effective on June 1, 1774. Parliament used British navy ships to block the port of Boston. The port would not be opened again for trade until the colonists paid the East India Company for the tea they dumped into the water. The act also required colonists to pay the British government taxes on the ruined tea.

The Boston Port Act also removed Boston as the capital of Massachusetts. Salem became the new capital, and the colony's main port became nearby Marblehead. This parliamentary action punished those living in the Boston area for having participated in the tea party. It resulted in financial hardship for people whose income was dependent on trade.

The British parliament wasn't finished passing laws that attempted to keep the colonists under its control. Two additional measures were introduced to Parliament on April 15, 1774. These were the Massachusetts Government Act and the Administration of Justice Act. Members of the British parliament did not support these acts as strongly as they had supported the Boston Port Act. Yet, despite some opposition, Parliament passed both of them. The king signed both into effect on May 20, 1774.

The Massachusetts Government Act took much governmental control from the colonists. It transferred this power to the British governor there. Under the act, the governor would appoint the

Boston's State House, also known as the "Towne House," was built in 1713. It served as a gathering place as well as the office of Boston's governors. Today it is the oldest building in Boston. It now serves as a history museum.

Massachusetts Council. The assembly of colonists would no longer elect the council. The governor would appoint all Massachusetts's law officers. The act also stated that the colonists' town meetings could only be held if the governor approved. Giving the governors more authority gave Parliament tighter control over the colonists.

The Administration of Justice Act stated that British officials serving in the colonies could not be tried for capital crimes there. The governor could move trials to different colonies or even to England to ensure the officials received a fair trial. To the colonists, this meant that the officials could do as they pleased and not fear justice.

The colonists resented both of these acts. The acts meant that more of the colonists' freedoms were falling under the control of the British government.

Parliament handed down other laws that impacted all of the colonies. One of these was the Quartering Act of June 2, 1774. Like the Quartering Act of 1765, it required the colonists to provide housing, food, and transportation for British troops in the colonies. Parliament felt the colonists should pay these expenses since the troops protected them from the French. The colonists did not feel threatened by the French. They did not want the British troops present in the colonies, nor did they want to cover the soldiers' living expenses. The colonists considered this act to be an indirect tax.

Parliament passed the Quebec Act on June 22, 1774. It became effective on May 1, 1775. This act gave the French Canadians of Quebec the freedom to practice Roman Catholicism. It also granted them their own government. The British government gave the Quebec settlers additional land in the Midwest. While the French colonists eagerly accepted this land, the American colonists were outraged. They felt that the land was theirs.

This act improved England's relationship with the French in Quebec. It worsened England's already tense relationship with the colonists. The British parliament knew that the colonists might eventually revolt against its authority. If a war broke out, the British wanted French support.

The Intolerable Acts of 1774 pushed the colonists to their limits. More colonists refused to live under the harsh British rules. Protests increased in the colonies. It seemed that revolution would only be a matter of time.

THE PUSH FOR INDEPENDENCE

The colonists resented the way Parliament was trying to control their lives. Boston colonists suffered financial hardship after Parliament closed their city's harbor. The citizens in the other colonies feared the same fate.

The colonists knew that they would be stronger if they banded together throughout the colonies. They decided to form a united voice of opposition against Parliament's actions.

The colonists formed an assembly to discuss the Intolerable Acts. This assembly was similar to the one formed in 1765 to oppose the Stamp Act. Members from the colonies were invited to find a solution to the problems facing them.

This assembly was called the First Continental Congress. It met from September 5 to October 26, 1774. Representatives from every colony except Georgia attended. They met in Carpenter Hall, in the city of Philadelphia. Peyton Randolph, from Williamsburg, Virginia, was elected president of this congress.

Members of the First Continental Congress voiced their opposition to Parliament's policies. A few suggested breaking away from England. Most members of the group did not believe the problems that existed between the colonists and England warranted the break. They favored working toward a peaceful negotiation.

The congress listed its requests and John Dickinson wrote them down. The requests were sent to England. The congress hoped to open a discussion with Parliament and reach an agreement. Members of this group agreed to meet again in May if Parliament did not change its policies.

Before May arrived, the relationship between the 13 colonies and England had grown worse. Some British troops were positioned in the colonies. The British navy patrolled the colonies' shores, and more troops were on the way from Europe.

The British government declared it would bring the colonists into submission. British soldiers and the colonists fought at Lexington and Concord on April 19, 1775. These battles marked the beginning of the American Revolutionary War.

A meeting of the First Continental Congress

FAMOUS WORDS

JOHN ADAMS, REVOLUTIONIST:
"The people should never rise without doing something to be remembered, something notable and striking. This destruction of the tea is so bold, so daring, so firm . . . and it must have so important consequences, and so lasting, that I can't but consider it an epoch in history."

SAMUEL ADAMS, REVOLUTIONIST:
"Tea stands for Tyranny!"

KING GEORGE III OF ENGLAND:
"Once vigorous measures appear to be the only means left of bringing the Americans to a due submission to the mother country, the colonies will submit."

ABIGAIL ADAMS, WIFE OF JOHN ADAMS:
"The tea, that baneful weed, is arrived. . . . The flame is kindled, and like lightning it catches from soul to soul . . . I tremble when I think what may be the direful consequences, and in this town [of Boston] must the scene of action lie. My heart beats at every whistle I hear, and I dare not express half my fears."

The Second Continental Congress met in Philadelphia for the first time on May 5, 1775. The group included now famous patriots Sam Adams, John Adams, Benjamin Franklin, John Hancock, Patrick Henry, and George Washington. Peyton Randolph of Virginia again was president. This assembly had some important decisions to make.

Some of the representatives believed it was time for the colonists to break from England. They believed that the presence of British troops on their land was further reason to fight for freedom. Yet, the congress was unable to pay for its own military. It could only write soldiers notes promising to pay them for their service later. Most doubted whether these notes had any real value.

Other members of the congress believed that the colonists still owed loyalty to England. They resented taxation without representation but felt it was their duty to handle the matter in a peaceful way. They wanted to find a solution without breaking ties with England.

Representatives of the First Continental Congress had supported opposing sides of the debate, too. But now, more and more delegates were looking toward independence as the proper solution to their problem.

Those searching for independence began to prepare for a larger war. The congress passed the Declaration of Causes of Taking up Arms. This document named England as the attacker. It said that the colonists had the right to arm themselves against the British threat.

The colonists established the Continental army and named George Washington its commander in chief. Benjamin Franklin traveled to France to establish a colonial alliance with the French. It took more than a year, but a treaty with France was finally reached.

George Washington

38

The colonists who favored peace decided to give diplomatic negotiations another try. A formal request was drafted and signed by members of the Continental Congress in July 1775. It was called the Olive Branch Petition. They sent the petition to King George III in England. It told King George III that the colonies were loyal to him. It also said that the colonies hoped a peaceful solution to the current conflict could be found. The colonists even offered suggestions.

King George III refused to read the Olive Branch Petition. He said that it was an illegal document created by an illegal congress. When representatives in the colonies heard that King George III had refused to read the petition, they were outraged.

For more than six years, the colonists fought for their freedom from England. The independent spirit of the American colonists triumphed over British domination in the Revolutionary War—just as it had during the Boston Tea Party.

A scene from the Revolutionary War

This 1776 map of Boston and its surrounding areas was drawn in pen, ink, and watercolor.

It was common for historical events, such as the American Revolutionary War, to trigger an increase in mapmaking.

Typically, maps like this one displayed military information. While these maps were not known for their accuracy, they provided helpful information to those engaged in war.

TIMELINE

 1763 France is defeated by British troops and colonial militia in the French and Indian War.

 1764 Parliament passes the American Revenue Act, also known as the Sugar Act.

Boston colonists form the Committee of Correspondence.

 1765 Parliament passes the Stamp Act and the Quartering Act.

Colonial delegates meet in New York for the Stamp Act Congress.

1766 The Stamp Act is repealed.

1767 The Townshend Acts are enacted.

 1768 British soldiers are stationed in Boston.

1770 British troops open fire on American colonists in the Boston Massacre.

 1773 The Tea Act is passed by Parliament.

On December 16, American colonists dump thousands of pounds of tea into Boston Harbor at the Boston Tea Party.

On December 17, Paul Revere rides to New York and Philadelphia spreading news of the tea party.

 1775 Battles at Lexington and Concord are fought on April 19.

1783 American colonists and Great Britain sign a peace treaty.

American Moments

FAST FACTS

From about 1500 to 1700, many European countries operated under an economic policy called mercantilism.

For more than 100 years, the relationship between Parliament and the American colonists was cooperative.

King George III ruled Great Britain and Ireland from 1760 until 1820. He, more than other monarchs before him, tried to control the colonies.

The Sons of Liberty encouraged fellow colonists to show their anger toward Parliament by rioting.

About 150 colonists disguised themselves and took part in the Boston Tea Party on December 16, 1773.

Paul Revere spread news of the Boston Tea Party when he traveled by horseback to New York and Philadelphia with a report of the night's events.

Parliament responded to the Boston Tea Party by implementing a series of laws that the colonists called the Intolerable Acts.

Georgia was the only colony that did not send delegates to the First Continental Congress in 1774. The colony was so dependent upon England's support that it did not want to offend Parliament and risk losing that support.

Famous patriots participated in the Second Continental Congress. Members included: Samuel Adams, John Adams, Benjamin Franklin, John Hancock, Patrick Henry, and George Washington.

WEB SITES
WWW.ABDOPUB.COM

Would you like to learn more about the Boston Tea Party? Please visit **www.abdopub.com** to find up-to-date Web site links about the Boston Tea Party and other American moments. These links are routinely monitored and updated to provide the most current information available.

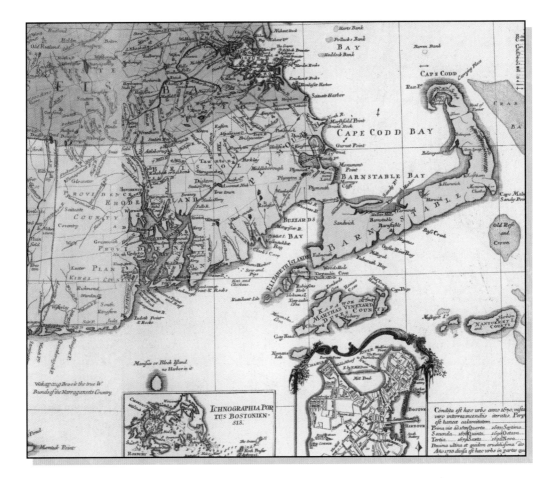

A map of colonial Massachusetts from the late 1700s

GLOSSARY

boycott: to refuse to deal with a person, store, or organization until they agree to certain conditions.

capital crime: a serious offense.

denomination: a religious organization that unites local churches into a single governing body.

House of Burgesses: colonial Virginia's lower house of the legislature.

indigo: blue dye made from plants.

militia: a group of citizens trained for combat during war or emergencies.

molasses: the thick, brown syrup produced when sugarcane is processed into sugar.

negotiation: the process of communicating with one or more people in order to reach an agreement.

parliament: the highest lawmaking body of some governments.

petition: to make a formal request to a person of authority.

repeal: to formally withdraw or cancel.

Ben Franklin was as well known for his patriotism as he was for his inventions. He convinced Parliament to repeal the despised Stamp Act.

INDEX